Nam Medieval Character:
Medieval Christian Names (12th-13th Centuries)

Name Your Medieval Character:
Medieval Christian Names (12th–13th Centuries)

Compiled by
Joyce DiPastena

Sable Tyger Books

Cover Design by Laura J. Miller
http://www.anauthorsart.com
Sable Tyger Logo by Lisa A. Messegee

Sable Tyger Books
Mesa, Arizona, USA
sabletygerbooks@gmail.com

Copyright 2013 Joyce DiPastena

All rights reserved. No portion of this work may be reproduced in print or electronically, other than brief excerpts for the purpose of reviews, without the written permission of the publisher.

ISBN: 978-0-9892419-2-2

OTHER WORKS BY JOYCE DiPASTENA

Books:

Loyalty's Web
Illuminations of the Heart
Dangerous Favor

Short Stories:

A Candlelight Courting: A Short Christmas Romance
"Caroles on the Geen," in *A Timeless Romance Anthology*: Winter Edition (2012)
An Epiphany Gift for Robin

Praise for Joyce DiPastena's books

"She puts you right into the dungeons and castle halls of France." Amazon reviewer

"Joyce does a wonderful job of portraying the medieval setting through visual and vocal details so you feel as though you are there." Martha's Bookshelf

"Every story I read, written by Joyce DiPastena, makes me fall in love with this time period more and more. Medieval France is brought to life again." Amazon reviewer

Introduction

As an author of medieval historical novels, I am always on the lookout for authentic medieval Christian names for my characters. Internet searches are helpful, but occasionally they can lead a writer astray. For example, some internet lists include literary names that were popularized at a much later date, but never in actual use during the Middle Ages. Ophelia is one such example. Shakespeare plucked it from a 15th Century poem for the tragic heroine of his play, ***Hamlet***. It became a popular girl's name in the 19th Century, but was not a name given to little girls by medieval parents.

Sometimes place names pop up as a medieval name suggestion. An example of this is Avalon for a girl's name. Avalon is, indeed, very pretty, but it is the name of an island in the legends of King Arthur and was never used in the Middle Ages as a person's first name.

Other lists extrapolate to modern spellings that

would have struck medieval parents as quite odd in their search for a name for their baby. An example of this is Chad. Chad derives from a seventh-century saint, Ceadda. Parents often named their children for saints and therefore might have named a male child Ceadda, but they would never have spelled his name Chad. Another consideration is that Ceadda is a Saxon name, which for the most part died out of use in England after the Norman Conquest. So you would not want to have a full-blooded Norman running around England (or Normandy) bearing the name Ceadda, and especially not the name Chad.

Additional "medieval" names I have seen on internet lists include Xena, Tasha, Queena, Gloriana, Taylor (an occupation and surname, never a person's first name) and on and on it goes … inaccurately.

Can you see the difficulty?

Accurate lists can be found on the internet, but it can take a deal of searching and double-checking of sources.

In ***Name Your Medieval Character: Medieval Christian Names (12th-13th Centuries)***, I have done much of this work for you. *Name Your Medieval Character* is a compilation of my 30-plus years of research into medieval Christian names.

Name Your Medieval Character

I have read books on name origins and studied the indexes of multiple historical resource books, painstakingly creating a roster of male and female Christian names that were cited in contemporary 12th and 13th Century historical records. In other words, every name and name variation in this book was borne by a living, breathing medieval man or woman.

My focus for this book is England and France in the 12th-13th centuries (since that is the setting of my historical novels), but I also have a smattering of names that precede and postdate these boundaries, as well as occasional names from other countries used during the same time period. In such cases, I have labeled names accordingly. (German, Italian, Scots, Welsh, etc. Saxon names generally preceded the Norman Conquest of 1066, though when a name survived into the Norman period, that is also noted.)

The reason some names have so many variations is because spelling had not yet become standardized, so the same person's name could be spelled multiple ways on multiple records. However, if you are a novelist, I would suggest using only one spelling per character to avoid confusion for modern-day readers.

Why have I included only Christian names, and not surnames, in this book? Because the use of surnames was still very much in flux in Europe during these centuries. A person might, in fact, be called by multiple surnames during his lifetime or even have no surname at all. But every person was given a Christian (first) name at birth and was consistently known by that name throughout his or her life.

Name Your Medieval Character includes over 800 female names (including variations) and over 1500 male names (including variations). That the male list is longer than the female list is, of course, a result of fewer women being named in historical records than men.

I hope my lists will be helpful to historical purists, fantasy writers, gamers, or anyone who just enjoys names!

Name Your Medieval Character

Explanation of notation following names

Most of the names on these lists were brought to England by the Norman Conquest of 1066. Therefore, I have not notated names that were specifically Norman. Names that were not Norman I have sought to notate. For example, (Saxon) following a name indicates that name preceded the Norman Conquest of England. Many Saxon names undoubtedly continued for some time among the lower, conquered classes (including serfs) after 1066. Over time, however, even the lower classes increasingly adopted Norman names. Since the focus of this book is the 12th and 13th Centuries, I have limited the number of Saxon names included in this volume. When a Saxon name survived into the 12th Century and later, I have noted that. **Example: Cuthbert (Saxon, survived Norman Conquest)**

Be aware that names brought to England by the Normans were obviously also used in

Normandy, and can therefore be safely used for novels set in and around that duchy.

If a name entered popularity after the 12th Century, I have notated that.

A notation such as (12-15 C) indicates that a name was popular in England from the 12-15 Centuries, and likely became less popular after the 15th Century. **Example: Aline (12 C-15 C)**

(<French) indicates that the name preceding this notation is a French (or Welsh or Italian, etc) version of the first name on the line. **Example: Margaret, Margherita (<Italian), Margiad (<Welsh), Marguerite (<French), Margot (<French)**

If a name was used strictly in Wales (or another country) the notation will simply be (Welsh). **Example: Gwenllian (Welsh)**

(<dim) indicates the name preceding this notation is a diminutive (shortened, pet or nickname) form of the name. **Example: Richard, Diccon (<dim)**

The word "popular" after a name indicates that this was a popular name among the Normans, both in Normandy and England.

"Rare", of course, is the opposite of the notation

Name Your Medieval Character

"popular." Such a name was occasionally used, but was not used frequently.

Sometimes a name had variations that began with different letters. **Example: Adelin, Edelin**. In these cases, I have listed the second version of the name (Edelin) under both "A" and "E", with the "E" version preceded by a * and followed by a notation such as: ***Edelin (see Adelin)**. The * indicates that a name is a spelling variation that appears in two places in the lists. This is for the convenience of readers who may be searching for names that begin with a specific letter who may not think to check an A name for an E variation.

The rest of my notations should be self-explanatory.

Medieval Male Names

Name Your Medieval Character

Names beginning with A and their variation

Absalom, Absolon (12-14 C)

Acelin, Acelet, Ascelin (popular, 13 C)

Adam

*Adred, Ailred, Alret (Saxon, see Ethelred)

Adrian (rare)

Alan, Alain, Alein, Allen, Allan, Alun

Alard, Adelard, Aylard, Alart

Alban (13 C)

Alberic, Alberi, Auberi, Aubrey

Albert, Alubert, Halbert

Aldred, Eldrid (Saxon)

Aldus, Aldis, Aldous (Saxon, continued through 13 C)

Aldwin, Aldin (Saxon)

Alexander, Alysaundre, Alesaunder

Aelfgar (Saxon)

Aethelric (Saxon)

Aelthewig (Saxon)

*Ailbert, Ailbriht, Ailbric, Albrict (Saxon, see Ethelbert)

Ailred

Aldred (Saxon)

Alfred, Alfrid, Alvere, Auvere, Alvery, Avery

Algar (Saxon)

Almeric, Americ, Emeric, Aimeri, Amaury, Amery, Aymor

Alric, Alaric, Ailric

Alwyn, Aylwin, Alewyn, Ailwyn

Amalric

Amfrid, Amfrey (to 14 C)

Amis (12-15 C)

Amleth

Amyas, Amiot (12-13 C rare)

Name Your Medieval Character

Ancel, Ancelin, Ancelot (a favorite Norman name)

Andrew

Aneurin, Aneirin (Welsh)

Ansgar

Anthony, Antony (<popular medieval form), Anton

Archard

*Armant, Armand (<French), Armin (<English) (see Herman)

Arnold, Arnoald, Arnald, Arnaud, Arnaut, Arnott, Ernald

Arnulf, Arnulph, Arnoul

*Arold (see Harold)

Arthur, Artor, Artur

Aubrey

*Auger (see Ogier)

Aumary, Amaury, Amery

Avenel

Averil, Everild

Aylmer (popular)

Aymer, Aymar

Name Your Medieval Character

Names beginning with B and their variations

Baldric, Baldri, Baudri, Baudry, Baudrey

Baldwin, Bawden, Boden, Balduin, Bowden

Bardolph, Bardell

Barnabas, Barnabe, Barnaby (11 C on)

Barret, Berold, Berolt

Bartholomew, Bartlet, Bartle, Bat

Basil, Basill

Batolf, Botulf, Botolfe

Benedict, Bennet, Beneyt

Benjamin (very rare)

Berenger, Bereniger, Benger (popular)

Bernard, Barnard, Barnet (popular)

Bernier

Bertram, Bertrand, Bertran, Bartram

Bevis, Beves, Bovo, Bob (popular)

Joyce DiPastena

Blanche, Blanch

Brand (Saxon)

Brian, Bryan, Brior (Irish and Breton)

Brice, Bryce, Bricot (Breton, brought to England by Normans, popular 13-14 C)

Bruno, Brun (Norman Conquest – 13 C)

Burthred

ଊଈ

Name Your Medieval Character

Names beginning with C and their variations

Cadwallader, Cadwalladr (Welsh)

*Canrice (Irish, see Kenneth)

Caradoc (Welsh)

Cecil

*Cennydd (Welsh, see Kenneth)

Cenred (Saxon)

Cerdic

Charles, Carle, Charlet (rare)

Chauncy, Chauncey (13 C on)

Christopher, Kester, Kit <dim>, Kett, Ketel (11 C on)

Clarence

Clement, Clemens, Clem, Clim

Clerebold, Clarenbald (11-14 C England)

Conal, Conall

Conan, Kynan (brought from Brittany after Norman Conquest)

Conrad (10 C)

Constantine, Costin, Costaine, Costane (11 C)

Cornelius (popular in low countries)

Corwin

Cosmo, Cosimo (favorite name in Italy)

Crispin, Crispian (from 13 C)

Curtis, Curteis

Cuthbert (Saxon, survived Norman Conquest)

*Cynric (Saxon, see Kenric)

Cyprian, Cyprianus (13 C)

Name Your Medieval Character

Names beginning with D and their variations

Damien, Damian (13 C)

Daniel, Danyell, Danyll

David (after Norman Conquest, popular 12 C)

Denis, Dionisius, Dynsius (11 C)

Derek, Derrick (15 C England)

*Dick(<dim), Diccon (<dim) (see Richard)

*Dob (<dim, see Robert)

*Dodge (see Roger)

Dominic, Dominick (13 C, rare in England)

Donatus, Donnet, Donat (<Irish), Dunawd (<Welsh)

Dougal, Dugald (Old Irish)

Drogo, Druet, Drew, Drue, Dreux (introduced by Norman Conquest)

Duncan (<Irish, Scots), Donecan

Dunstan, Donestan, Dunestan (11 C on)

Joyce DiPastena

Durand, Durant (introduced by Normans)

ぐぞう

Name Your Medieval Character

Names beginning with E and their variations

Eadmer (Saxon)

Edgar, Etgar (Saxon, rare after Norman Conquest)

Edmund, Edmond (popular)

Edred, Eadred (Saxon)

Edric (Saxon)

Edward, Edouard (<French), Eduard (<German) (popular)

Edwin, Eaduin (Saxon, rare after 13 C)

Egbert (Saxon, rare after Norman Conquest)

*Eldrid (Saxon, see Aldred)

Elijah, Elias, Elis, Elys (popular in Middle Ages)

Emery, Emeric, Emerick (introduced by Normans, rare)

*Enguerran, Enguerrand, Engelard (see Ingram)

*Eoin (Irish for of John, see Sean)

*Eral (see Harold)

Eric (introduced by Danes)

*Ernald (see Arnold)

Ernost

Esmond (rare, died out 14 C)

Ethelbert, Ailbert, Ailbriht, Ailbric, Albert, Albrict (Saxon)

Ethelred, Edred, Adred, Ailred, Alret (Saxon)

Etienne

Eudes, Eudo

Eduo, Eudes, Eudon, Udo

Eustace, Eustache, Eustas, Ewistace

*Evan (<Welsh), Ewan (<Scots) (see John)

*Evein, Ywein, Yvain (Welsh, see Owen)

Evelin

Everard, Everitt, Everet

Name Your Medieval Character

*Everild (see Averil)

಩಩

Names beginning with F and their variations

Faramond

Felix, Felis, Felyse

Fergus (Scots and Irish)

Ferrand, Ferant, Ferrant

*Fithian (12 C, fairly popular, see Vivian)

Florence

Florian

Frank, Franco, Fraunk (somewhat popular)

Fulbert, Filbert

Fulk, Fauke, Fowke, Fawke, Fulcher (popular)

Name Your Medieval Character

Names beginning with G and their variations

Gabriel, Gabrell, Gabryell (rare)

Galen

Galeran

*Garnier, Gerner, Garner (fairly popular 12-14 C, see Warner)

Gamelyn

Gareth, Gahariet (Welsh)

Garin

Gawain, Gawyne, Gawyn, Gawin, Gawen, Gavin, Gawne (fairly popular)

Geoffrey, Geffrey, Geffroi, Geffrei, Geffrai, Jaufre (popular 12-15 C)

George (earliest example end of 12 C, occasional 13-14 C)

Geraint (Welsh)

Gerald, Gerolt, Geroldin, Garoux (died out end of 13 C)

Gerard, Gairhard, Gyrerd, Garrett, Garrat, Garit, Girard (popular)

Gerbert

Gerbold, Gerbod (fairly popular)

Geré (Norman)

Geri, Gerwy

German, Jerman, Jarman, Jermyn (fairly popular)

Gervais, Gervase, Gervis, Jarvis

Giffard, Gyffard, Gifford (popular, 11-12 C)

Gilbert, Gylbart, Gylbard, Gilbred, Gulbert, Guibert (popular)

Giles, Gilles, Gylis, Gilo, Gilius

*Giovanni (<Italian, see John)

Girars

Glyn (Welsh)

Godfrey

Goldwin, Godwine (fairly popular)

Name Your Medieval Character

Goronwy (Welsh)

Gorwy

Goscelin

Granville, Grenville

Gregory, Gregour (popular)

Griffin, Griffith, Gruffudd, Gruffydd (Welsh)

Grimbald, Grimbaud, Grimbol, Grimold (fairly popular)

*Gualter (see Walter)

Gueri

Guerric, Garin

*Guichard (<French, see Richard)

*Guilielm, Gillet, Gillot, Gilliame, Guillot, Gilmyn, Guillaume (<French) (see William)

Guiscard, Wiscard

Gunter (13-14 C)

Guy, Guyon, Guise, Wy, Wyon

Joyce DiPastena

Gyrth (Saxon)

Name Your Medieval Character

Names beginning with H and their variations

*Hab (<Scots, dim for Robert), *Hob (<dim for Robert)

Hacon, Hacun, Hacon (introduced by Danes)

*Halbert (see Albert)

Hamo, Hamon, Haymo, Hamund, Hamelin

*Hans (German, see John)

Hardwin (popular till 13 C)

Harold, Harald, Arold, Herald, Heral, Eral, Herolt

Harvey, Haerveu (<Breton), Hervi (12-14 C)

Hector (13 C)

Helie, Helias

Henry, Hanry, Harry, Harrich, Herry, Henri, Heriot (<dim French), Herriot (<dim French)

Herluin, Herlwin

Herbert, Herebert, Harbert (popular until 13 C)

Hereward (Saxon, survived till end of 13 C)

Herman, Harman (<Norman), Armant, Armand (<French), Armin (<English)

Hervé, Hervey, Hervis

Hilary, Hilaire (French, 13-16 C)

Hildebrand, Hildebrant (fairly popular, 13-14 C)

Hippolytus, Ippolitus, Ypolitus (13-14 C)

*Hodge, Hotch (see Roger)

*Holiver (see Oliver)

*Hotys (see Odo)

Howell (<Welsh), Hoel (<English)

Hubert, Hubard, Hobard

Hugh, Hugo, Hughes, Hugon (<N French); Hue, Huon (<S French)

Humphrey, Humbrye, Humbrey, Onfroi, Umbray

Name Your Medieval Character

Hywel (Welsh)

◊

Names beginning with I and their variations

Iefan, Ifan, Yevan

Ilbert

Imbert, Isembert, Imbart

Ingram, Ingelram, Enguerran, Enguerrand, Engelard

Iolo (Welsh)

Isenbart

Ivo, Ives, Yves, Yvo, Ivone, Yvone

Ivor, Ifor (Irish, Scots, and Welsh)

☙❧

Name Your Medieval Character

Names beginning with J and their variations

James, Jacque (13 C)

*Jarvis (see Gervais)

Jaspar, Jesper (<English, 14 C),

Kaspar (<German), Gaspard (<French), Gaspar (<Spanish), Gaspare (<Italy)

*Jaufre (popular 12-15 C, see Geoffrey)

Jeremy (13 C)

*Jerman, Jarman, Jermyn (fairly popular, see German)

Jerome, Jeronim

Jevon, Jevan, Yevan

John, Jack (<dim), Jankin (<dim), Jean (<French), Evan (<Welsh), Ewen (<Scots), Eoin (<Irish), Sean (<Irish), Hans (<German), Giovanni (<Italian)

Jonathon (occasionally, 13 C)

Jordan (end 12 C)

Joyce DiPastena

Joseph (rare)

Jocelin

Joyce, Jocea, Jossy, Jocey (also female)

Julian, Jolin

Name Your Medieval Character

Names beginning with K and their variations

Kenelm, Kenhelm

Kenneth, Cennydd (<Welsh), Canrice (<Irish)

Kenric, Kenrick, Cynric (Saxon)

Kenwarad (<Saxon), Kenard (<Anglo-Norman)

Kevin (Irish)

*Kester, Kett, Ketel, Kit (<dim of Christopher>) (11 C on, see Christopher)

*Kickon (<dim, see Richard)

*Kynan (brought from Brittany after Norman Conquest, see Conan)

Names beginning with L and their variations

Lambert, Lambard, Lamberkin, Lambin

Lancelin, Lance, Lancelot, Lencelin, Lancelyn, Lanslet

Laurence, Lawrence

Leofric, Leuric, Leouric, Lefric, Leferich, Lefrich (Saxon, survived Norman Conquest)

Leofstan (Saxon)

Leofwine (Saxon)

Leon, Lyon, Leo, Leonidem

Leonard

Lewis, Louis, Lowis, Llewelyn (<Welsh), Aloys (<Provençal), Aloisio (<Provençal)

Lionel, Leonel, Lyonell

Llewellyn, Llewelyn (<Welsh),

Leolin (<Anglicized), Leolline (<Anglicized)

Lovell, Lovet, Lovel

Name Your Medieval Character

Lucian

Luke, Lukas, Lucas

Lyulf, Lyulph, Lyolf, Liulf, Ligulf

ଓଽଠ

Names beginning with M and their variations

*Mace (French, <dim of Thomas), Macey (French, <dim of Thomas)

Madoc, Maddoc (Welsh)

Malcolm (Scots, occasionally England)

Manfred

Marmaduke, Marmaduc (chiefly in York)

Martin, Martyn

Matthew, Matthais, Mathieu, Matheu, Machin, Machon, Mathiu

Mauger, Malger, Margre

Maurice, Meurisse, Moris, Morris, Meurik, Morys, Mourice, Mauris

Maynard, Mainard

Meiler

Mervyn (Welsh)

Name Your Medieval Character

Michael, Mighel, Mikael, Michel (<French)

Miles, Milo, Milon

Morcar (Saxon)

Morgan (Welsh)

Mortain

Murdoch

Marcus, Mark, Marke

Names beginning with N and their variations

Neville, Neuville, Nevil, Nevell

Nicholas, Nicol, Nicolin, Nicolet, Nick, Nochole, Nycolas

Nigel, Niall, Neil (all Irish), Nel, Nele (Norman), Neel

Niger

*Nob (<dim for Robert)

Noel, Nowell (for a child born on Christmas)

Norman, Normand

Name Your Medieval Character

Names beginning with O and their variations

Odo, Otho, Oddo, Otto, Otho, Odinel, Ode, Odde, Hotys

Odelin

Ogier, Oger, Oggery, Auger

Oliver, Olivier, Holiver, Olver, Ollier (<Breton)

*Onfroi (see Humphrey)

Osbert (Northumbrian name)

Osborn, Osberne, Osbarn

Oscar, Osgar (Irish)

Osmond, Osmund, Osman, Osment, Osmint, Osmen Osmand

Osric

Oswald, Osewold, Osuald, Oswold, Oswell, Oswall

Oswin

Joyce DiPastena

Owen, Owain, Owayne, Ouen, Ouein, Owyn, Owyne, Evein, Ywain, Ywein, Yvain, Uwen (Welsh)

Name Your Medieval Character

Names beginning with P and their variations

Pagan, Payn, Payne, Pagane, Pannet, Paganel, Paynel

Pascoe, Pask, Pascal, Pasche

Patrick (<Irish, Scots, N England), Paterick, Patrycke, Pattrik

Paulin, Pawlin

Perceval, Percival (invented by Chretien de Troyes in 12 C)

Peregrine (13 C)

Peter, Piers (<French), Petur, Petyr, Perote, Peres, Peirce, Perrin (<dim), Perkin (<dim), Parkin (<dim), Perott (<dim), Perot, (<dim>), Perrot (<dim)

Philip, Phelippe, Phelyp, Phelypp, Phylypp, Philkin (<dim)

*Phythian, Fithian (12 C, fairly popular, see Vivian)

Picot

Joyce DiPastena

Names beginning with Q and their variations

Quentin, Quintin (11-13 C)

Name Your Medieval Character

Names beginning with R and their variations

Raimbaut

Ralph, Rauf, Raff, Raulf, Radulf, Raff, Rauffe, Riolf

Randal, Ranulf, Rand, Rankin, Randolph, Rannulf

Raoul, Raoulin, Raoulet, Rawlin, Raulyn

Raymond, Raimund, Reimund

Rayner, Rainer, Raynor, Reyner

Raynold, Reinald, Reynaud, Rainald, Renaut, Reynald

Reginald, Rainbald, Regnaut

Rene, René

Renfred, Reimfred, Reynfrey, Remfrey

Reynard, Rainard

Rhydderch (Welsh)

Rhys, Reece, Rice

Richard, Richart, Richer, Ricard, Rick (<dim), Dick(<dim), Diccon (<dim), Kickon (<dim), Guichard (<French)

Robert (Rob, Hob, Dob, Nob, all <dim), Robin (<dim), Robard, Robyn (<dim), (Rab, Hab, <dim, Scots), Rab, Roy (<dim, Irish)

Rodulf

Roger, Rodger, Hodge, Dodge, Hotch

Roland, Rowland, Rouland, Rolland

Rolf, Rolfe, Rolph, Rollo, Rolle, Roulf

Roncelin

Rory (Irish)

Roscelin

Rotrou

Roussel

Ruald

Name Your Medieval Character

Names beginning with S and their variations

Saer, Sayer, Sagar, Sagard

Samson, Sampson, Sanson, Sansum

Samuel (rare)

Savary, Savaric

Sean (Irish), Eoin (Irish) (both forms of John)

Serle, Serlo, Serill

Seumus (Irish for James)

Sewal (Saxon), Sewale (Saxon)

Siffroi

Silvester, Sylvester, Silvestre (first noted in 1200)

Simeon, Shimeon, Symeon

Simon, Simond, Symon, Symounde, Symkyn, Symme

Siward, Syward, Seuard (pre-Norman thru 14 C)
Stephen, Stephan, Steven, Stevyn

Stigand (Saxon)

*Swalter (see Walter)

Swayn

Name Your Medieval Character

Names beginning with T and their variations

Talbot, Talebot

Tancred (uncommon in England)

Theobald, Teebald, Tebbe, Tebaud, Tebald, Tibbott, Tibald, Tetbald, Teobald

Theoderic, Teodric, Theodric, Tedric, Terry, Theirry, Terrick

Thomas, Thome, Thomasin, Thomelin, Tom, Thom, (Mace & Macey – French dim)

Thorold, Torold, Turold, Thorald

Thurstan, Thurstin, Turstan, Turstin, Thrystan

Tihel

Tobias, Toby, Tobye, Tobin, Tobyn

Toki (Saxon)

Torcail (<Scots), Torquil (survived 13 C)

Tristram, Tristan, Tristran, Trystrem, Tristian, Triston

Tybert

☙❧

Name Your Medieval Character

Names beginning with U and their variations

Uchtred, Ughtred, Uctred, Uhtred (Saxon, survived Norman Conquest)

*Udo (see Eudo)

Ulric, Wulurich, Wulfric, Ulfric (Saxon, survived Norman Conquest)

*Umbray (see Humphrey)

Urian, Urien, Uryene (Welsh, but also found in England)

*Uwen (see Owen)

Names beginning with V and their variations

Valentine

Valerian (13 C)

Victor (1200s, but rare)

Vincent (13 C)

Vitalis, Viel (Norman, not uncommon)

Vivian, Phythian, Fithian (12 C, fairly popular)

Vulgrin

Name Your Medieval Character

Names beginning with W and their variations

Walbert

Waleran

Walter, Wauter, Gualter, Swalter (a favorite Norman name)

Waltheof, Waldeve, Waldive, Waldeof, Waldief (Saxon, survived Norman Conquest)

Warner, Wariner, Garnier, Gerner, Garner (fairly popular 12-14 C)

Warren, Warin, Guarin (rare after 14 C)

Wilfred, Wilfrid (Saxon, rare after Norman Conquest)

William, Guilielm, Guillaume (<French), Willelm, Wylymot, Gillet, Gillot, Gilliame, Guillot, Gilmyn (William was THE most popular name in the Middle Ages)

*Wiscard (see Guiscard)

*Wulurich, Wulfric (Saxon, survived Norman Conquest, see Ulric)

*Wy, Wyon (see Guy)

Wystan, Wistan (Saxon)

☙❧

Name Your Medieval Character

Names beginning with Y and their variations

Ydain

*Yevan (see Iefan)

*Yevan (see Jevon)

Ysengrin

*Yves, Yvo, Yvone (see Ivo)

*Ywein, Yvain (Welsh, see Owen)

Medieval Female Names

Names beginning with A and their variations

Ada

Adama

Adela

Adelaide

Adelart

Adele, Adela

Adelin, Edelin

Adeliza (Norman)

Aelfled, Alfled(a), Alflet, Elfleda, Elflet (Saxon, rare after Norman Conquest)

Agatha, Agace, Agacia, Agase, Agas

Agnes, Agneta, Annis, Annys, Anneyce, Annot, Anhes

*Aileve (see Elgiva; Saxon, survived)

*Ala (see Ella)

Albreda, Albray, Aubrey

Name Your Medieval Character

Alda, Aude

Aldith, Ailith (Saxon)

Alice, Alesia, Alicia, Alys, Aelis, Ailsa

*Alienor, Alinor (see Eleanor)

Aline, Alina, Alyna (12 C-15 C)

Alison, Alicen (13 C on)

Alix

Amabel, Amabile Amble, Mabel (12-13 C, popular)

*Ameline (see Emmeline)

Amice, Amicia (popular 12-15 C)

Amicia

Amieria

Andrea

Ann, Anne, Nan, Nanny (rare)

Arabella, Orabell (rare)

Arta

Ascelina (popular, 13 C)

Athelinda, Athelyna (Saxon)

Audiart, Audiart

*Aveline, Avaline, Avelina, Avelyn (see Evelina)

Avice, Avis (Norman, 12-14 C)

ಆ

Name Your Medieval Character

Names beginning with B and their variations

Barbara, Barbary

Basilia, Basilie, Basilla (popular, 12-13 C)

Beata (12 C on, rare)

Beatrix, Beatrice, Beautrice, Bettrys (<Welsh), Beton (<dim) (12-13 C)

Benedicta, Benoite (13 C on)

Berengaria

Bertha, Berthe, Berta (to 14 C)

Bertrada

Blanche

Bridget, Brigit, Brigid, Bride, Bryde (Irish, 13 C)

Briseida (used in 12 C poem)

Bronwyn (Welsh)

Names beginning with C and their variations

Cassandra, Cassandry

*Catharine, Catherine, Caterine (<French), Cateline (<French), Catlin (see Katherine)

Cecilia, Cecily, Cicely, Cecile, Sisley, Cecillia

Ceridwen (Welsh)

Christine, Christina (rare)

Clara, Clare (13 C on)

Clarice, Claricia, Clarisse

Clarimond

Clarissa

Clemence, Clemency, Clemens (13 C on)

Clotho

Clotilda, Clotilde, Clothilde

Colette, Coletta, Coleta, Collette, Kalotte (13 C on)

Constance, Constantia, Custance, Custans

Name Your Medieval Character

Cornelia

Cressida

❧

Names beginning with D and their variations

Denise, Dennet, Diot, Dionisia, Dionycia

Diote

Donnat, Donnet

Dowsabel, Dowse, Duce, Douse (popular in Middle Ages)

Durande

Name Your Medieval Character

Names beginning with E and their variations

Edborough (Saxon, survived till 17 C)

*Edelin (see Adelin)

Edilda

Edith, Eadgyth, Editha, Eda, Edan (popular)

Egelina, Eglin, Agilina, Hegelina (13-14 C)

Eglentyne, Aiglente, Aiglentine

Eilian

Elinued

Ela

Eleanor, Elinor, Alienor, Alinor, Elianor

*Elfleda, Elflet (see Aelfled; Saxon, rare after Norman Conquest)

Elfreda, Elfrid (Saxon, rare after Norman Conquest)

Elgiva, Elveva, Aileve (Saxon, survived)

Elizabeth, Elizabet, Elise (<French), Lisette (<French), Elspeth <Scottish), Elspie (<Scottish) (occasionally used in 13-14 C; see **Isabel**)

Ella, Ela, Ala, Elia, Hele (popular to mid-14 C)

Ellen, Elena, Elene, Ellyn, Elen, Elot, Elota

Eluned, Luned (Welsh)

Emily, Emilie, Emilia, Emelye, Emulea

Emlyn (Welsh)

Emma, Emme, Emmote, Emmete

Emmeline, Ameline, Emlin, Emelina, Emelyn

*Emoni (see Ismena)

Ermengarde

*Essylt (Welsh, see Isolda)

Estrild (Saxon, survived until 12 C)

Etain (Irish)

Ethelburg, Ethelburga (Saxon)

Etheldred (Saxon)

Eugenia, Eugenie

Name Your Medieval Character

Euphemia, Eufemia, Eupheme, Femmota

Eustacia

Eva, Eve, Evota (from end of 12 C)

Evelina, Evelyn, Aveline, Avaline, Avelina, Avelyn

Evote

ଓଆଠ

Names beginning with F and their variations

Felicia, Felice, Felisia, Fillsia, Felis (end of 12 C)

*Femmota (see Euphemia)

Flora, Floria (13-14 C)

Florence, Flossie

Name Your Medieval Character

Names beginning with G and their variations

Galiena, Gaunleya, Ganleya, Gaunliena

Gemma

Gersendis

*Gille, Gylle (prounced with soft "g", see Julianna)

Gilliena, Galiana

Gillian, Gill, Jill, Gillot, Gillet (popular)

Gisela, Gisele (French)

Goda (Saxon)

*Gacelyn, Gascelin, Goslin (pronounced with soft "g", see Jacelyn)

Griflet

Guelfa

Guilhelma

Gunnilda (Saxon)

Gunnor (Saxon)

Gwenllian (Welsh)

Gytha

⚜

Name Your Medieval Character

Names beginning with H and their variations

*Hele (see Ella)

Hawise, Hawisia

Helewise, Helwise, Heloise

Helisen, Helisende

Helvie

Herleve

Hermeline

Hersent

Honora

*Hursel (see Ursula)

Hywelis (Welsh)

Joyce DiPastena

Names beginning with I and their variations

Ingrid, Ingrede, Ingerith (Old Norse)

Isabel, Isobel, Isabelle, Isabella, Isabeau, Ibbet, Ibota, Ysabel (Isabel and its variations were the usual English medieval form of Elizabeth)

Ismena, Ismenia, Ysmena, Imania, Emoni, Imanie

Isolda, Essylt (<Welsh), Isold, Isolt, Iseut (<French), Isaut (<French), Ysolt, Isota, Isylte

Ivette, Ivetta, Yvette

Name Your Medieval Character

Names beginning with J and their variations

Jacelyn, Jascelin, Joslin (also spelled with a G)

Jacoba

Jacqueline, Jacquetta, Jakolina, Jakelina, Jaclyn

Janeta, Jonet, Jennet

Jehane, Jean

*Jill (see Gillian)

Joan, Jehane, Jehhane (<French), Jhone, Johanna, Johna

*Jolenta, Joecia (see Yolande)

Joy, Joia, Johi, Hoiha, Joye (13 C)

Joyce, Jocea, Jossy, Jocey (also male)

Judith, Judita

Juet, Juetta, Julitta

Juliana, Julianna, Julian, Julyan, Gille, Gylle, Juet, Jelyan

෴

Name Your Medieval Character

Names beginning with K and their variations

*Kalotte (see Colette)

Katherine, Katharine, Catharine, Catherine, Caterine (<French), Cateline (<French), Katerine, Kateline, Catlin, Kateryne, Kateryn, Kytte, Kit, Kate

Names beginning with L and their variations

Lachesis

Laurencia, Lauretta, Laura, Lora (<end 12 C), Lore, Loretta

Lavina, Lavena

Leah

Leonia, Leonina

Lettice, Laetitia, Letice, Letyce, Lecelina, Lesceline, Lecia, Lece (<French)

Linnet, Lynnette

*Lisette (French; see Elizabeth)

Lucy, Luce, Lucie, Luciana, Lucette, Lucina, Lucia

*Luned (Welsh, see Eluned)

Name Your Medieval Character

Names beginning with M and their variations

*Mabel, Mabella, Mabilla, Mablia, Mably, Mab (see Amabel)

Madalena, Madeline, Madeleine, Madelina, Maudeleyn

Maeve

Malyne

Marcia

Marec

Margaret, Margareta, Margarete, Margarette, Markaret, Margat, Margyt, Margote, Meggot, Magge, Megge, Meg (<dim) Marguerite (<French), Margot (<French), Margherita (<Italian), Margiad (<Welsh)

Marina (14 C)

Marion, Mariane, Marianne, Marian

Marlen

Mary, Mariot, Moll, Mall, Mariota, Malkyn, Mariel, Mall

Mathe

Matilda, Maud, Maude, Mahild, Mahault, Molde, Mathilde, Mathild, Mathila Till (<dim), Tillot (<dim)

Meliora, Melior (Cornish name)

Millicent, Melicent, Malasintha, Melisende, Melisenda, Melisent, Melisant, Millicenta

Mirabel, Mirable, Marabel

Muriel, Meriel, Miriel, Muriella, Miriella, Mirield, Miriald

Mylisant, Melisende, Melusine

CR&O

Name Your Medieval Character

Names beginning with N and their variations

Nessie, Nesta (Welsh diminutive of Agnes)

Nicola, Nicolette, Nicholaa, Nicole

Nildred, Neldred

Noel, Nowell (for a child born on Christmas)

Norinna, Noirin (Irish)

Novella

☙❧

Names beginning with O and their variations

Odette, Odile, Odilia

Olimpe (French)

Olive, Olivia, Olyffe, Olyff, Olivet, Ollett

Olwen (Welsh)

Olyn, Olynne

Oriana

Oriel, Oriott, Oriolda, Oriholt

Osanne

Osthryth

Name Your Medieval Character

Names beginning with P and their variations

Patricia

Paula, Paulina, Pauline

Petronilla, Petronella, Petronyl, Peronel, Peternell, Petronel (Pernel & Parnel were generic names for a priest's concubine)

Philippa, Phillipa, Philippe

Philomena

Pleasance, Pleasant, Plesencia, Placencia, Plasancia (13 C)

Prudence, Prudencia, Prudentia (13 C)

Names beginning with R and their variations

Regina, Reina, Reine (<French)

Rhonwen (Welsh)

Richenda, Richarda, Richolda, Richilda, Richildis

Rosamund, Rosamond, Rosamunda, Rosemunda

Rose, Roese, Rohese, Rohaise, Royse, Roesia, Rohesia, Roysia, Rosa, Roseia

Rowena, Renwein, Ronwen

Name Your Medieval Character

Names beginning with S and their variations

Salerna

Sara, Sarah, Sarra

Savin, Sabyn, Sabina

Scholastica, Scholace, Scholast (13 C)

Serena

Sibyl, Sibylla, Sibilla, Sibilia, Sibilie, Sibell, Sibill, Sibota, Sybby, Sybyly

Sigrid, Sirida, Sierida, Sigerith (Scandanavian)

Siriol

*Sisley (see Cecilia)

Susan, Susannah (occasionally 13 C)

☙❧

Names beginning with T and their variations

Taddea

Theophania, Tifaine (<Old French), Teffany, Theffania, Thiffania, Thiphania, Tiffonia, Theofania, Tiffany, Teffan, Tyffany

Thomasin, Thomasine (mid-14 C)

*Till (<dim), Tillot (<dim) (see Mathilda)

Tura

Name Your Medieval Character

Names beginning with U and their variations

Ursula, Ursel, Ursell, Hursel, Urcy, Ursalay, Urseley

☙❧

Names beginning with V and their variations

Violette (<S French in Middle Ages, rare in England)

Vivianna

Name Your Medieval Character

Names beginning with W and their variations

Winifred, Wenefreda (Saxon)

Wymarca

Names beginning with Y and their variations

Yolande, Jolenta, Joecia

*Ysabel (see Isabel)

*Ysmena (see Ismena)

 *Ysolt (see Isolda)

*Yvette (see Ivette)

About the Author

Joyce DiPastena dreamed of green medieval forests while growing up in the dusty copper mining town of Kearny, Arizona. She filled her medieval hunger by reading the books of Thomas B. Costain (where she fell in love with King Henry II of England), and later by attending the University of Arizona where she graduated with a degree in history, specializing in the Middle Ages. The university was also where she completed her first full-length novel…set, of course, in medieval England. Later, her fascination with Henry II led her to expand her research horizons to the far reaches of his "Angevin Empire" in France, which became the setting of her first published novel, *Loyalty's Web* (a 2007 Whitney Award Finalist).

When she's not writing, Joyce loves to read, play the piano, and spend time with her sister and friends. A highlight of her year is attending the annual Arizona Renaissance Festival .

Joyce is a multi-published, multi-award winning author who specializes in sweet medieval romances heavily spiced with mystery and adventure. She lives with her two cats, Clio and Glinka Rimsky-Korsokov, in Mesa, Arizona.

Email her at jdipastena@yahoo.com

Read more about her books on her website at http://www.joyce-dipastena.com

See what she's working on now at http://jdp-news.blogspot.com

Follow along as she researches her books at http://medievalresearch.blogspot.com

You can also find her on Facebook (AuthorJoyceDiPastena) and Twitter (@JoyceDiPastena)

A Candlelight Courting: A Short Christmas Romance

A Candlelight Courting:
A Short Christmas Romance

(1st Place Honorable Mention, 2012 RONE Award by InD'Tale Magazine)

Meg has her heart set on becoming a nun. When Burthred comes courting on Christmas Eve, Meg rejects his advances and insists that he call her Christina, the spiritual name she has chosen for herself. She tries to make him swear on her box of holy relics that he will not pursue her, but he carefully words his oath to allow him to stay in her candlelit chamber and try to change her mind.

What Meg does not confess is that her reliquary box holds a secret.

Burthred needs a wife, and no one will satisfy him except Meg. He swore on his father's deathbed that he would marry her. But Burthred has a secret, too. When they come together before the Yule fire, their shared revelations will either join their hearts together or tear them apart.

Excerpt from *A Candlelight Courting*

England 1168 ~ Norgate Castle

Christina ran her thumb over the third smooth bead and repeated another Ave. Her parents had taken away her devotional table, with its carved crucifix and kneeling bench and a rest support for her arms while she repeated her rosary. They thought they had taken her rosary, too, but she had hidden a second one under her mattress.

"Hail Mary, full of grace . . . "

Her chamber's floor chafed her knees through her woolen skirts. Her parents had removed her prayer pillow, too. She should have thought to dispose of that comfort herself. The austerity her father viewed as punishment only prepared her for her chosen future. She had blessed him for the reminder and promptly blown out her candles and doused the coals in her brazier, as well. Her teeth chattered against the chill air that seeped through her gown's coarse fabric, but she pressed doggedly on with her prayer.

" . . . blessed art thou among women . . . "

Her voice pitched higher and louder as the

strains of the music swelled from the great hall of Norgate Castle below stairs, until her determination to drown out the competing noise nearly left her shouting. Why were they not singing solemn hymns on this holy night, instead of dancing like heathens? She had been compelled to attend enough of her father's Christmas feasts through the years to recognize the driving beat that thrummed the timbers of the floor as one of the lively carole dances Sir Alun was partial to.

She imagined her father roaring in his deep bass voice, "The holly and the ivy," as his heavy body lumbered around in an otherwise lightly skipping circle that included her mother and uncles and aunts and cousins and more meddlesome neighbors than she cared to number. "The rising of the sun, the running of the deer," they would sing in their turn in united refrain. When her uncle the abbot reproved them, they would widen their eyes and innocently deny the words held any pagan meanings, but rather a mystical symbolism so wise a priest as he could surely discern.

He had frowned at them for eighteen years, but this was the year she would prove his strictures had fallen on one pair of listening ears.

Her thumb moved to another bead. "Hail Mary, full of grace . . . "

She wondered if God objected to being bellowed at on Christmas Eve. Or to grumbling stomachs that rumbled a low counterpoint to

A Candlelight Courting

prayer.

Between the music, her determination to ignore her hunger, and her vociferous invocation, she did not hear the tread of footsteps outside her door. A sudden blast of pipe and drum warned her too late that someone had flung open the door. She sprang up from her knees and tucked her hands with the betraying rosary behind her back, thankful for the protective gloom that hid her motion. She wondered if she could cast herself onto her bed in pretended slumber before the intruder saw.

"Don't think you can fool me with this darkness," her father bellowed. "I heard you screeching through the door, so I know you're not asleep."

This time she heard the footfall that accompanied these words, followed by a thud and a howl. She had left her velvet-cushioned sitting stool just inside the threshold. On a celebratory night like this, Sir Alun would be wearing soft soled slippers, the sort that provided little protection against stubbed toes. With a curse, the hulking shadow that was her father swooped down and up again. Christina dodged just in time to avoid being struck as the stool sailed over her head and crashed with a great, splintering bang against the wall behind her bed.

"Devil take you, you contrary wench. If this were any other night of the year and your uncle not standing downstairs—"

It was nearly as dark outside the open doorway as it was inside her chamber, so she felt rather than saw the fist that checked just short of her nose. Christina flinched away. The one thing her father had never done yet was to strike her. But he had never thrown a stool over her head before, either.

"Light a candle," Sir Alun snapped, "and do what you came to do. I cannot explain away a bruised face to her uncle the abbot, but even he will understand the unsteadiness of women and the hot blood of youth. I'll have a meek, obedient daughter for Christmas Day."

He left as abruptly as he had arrived, his shadow vanishing behind the slammed door.

The sound reverberated in her ears as she struggled to calm her breathing. She had always known her father's patience must reach an end. If she could only speak to her uncle and convince him that her decision was irrevocable, the stern abbot would surely find a way to make possible this yearning that burned in her like a fever. She had thought to prove her resolve to him by shutting herself away from the Yule festivities that had set her eyes aglow as a child. Instead of partaking of the wassail cup and bread flavored with that divine, expensive spice called ginger that her father paid a merchant for but once a year, she had fasted on nothing but water and humdrum brown bread for a fortnight. But she belatedly realized should not have shut herself away in her bedchamber while she did so, for now she could not even speak to her uncle, and he would be gone the day after Christmas.

Unless . . . Had her father locked the door? She had not heard the distinctive click. She took a step forward to test the latch, then froze, the hairs prickling along the back of her neck. A sky heavy for weeks with snow clouds blocked even a faint glimmer of the stars or moon from filtering through the wooden shutters into her chamber. Even so, she could have found her way to the door with her eyes closed, but she felt her lids instead straining wide. She thought she heard a soft intake of breath. A breath that had not come from her lungs.

"Who's there?" Her voice came out in a terrified strangle.

A rustling sound, followed by a distinct clearing of a throat, and then, "My lady—"

The gruff male voice topped off her panic. Christina stumbled back against her bed and screamed like a madwoman.

"Meg, don't. It's just me, Burthred."

Just Burthred?

"Wh-what are you doing in my chamber? Why did my father—"

Oh, Saints, there could be only one reason he was here. She groped in the darkness and found one of the severed legs of the stool where it had fallen atop her bed. She clutched it up and waved it in front of her in warning.

"Don't you come near me."

"There's precious little chance of that, since I can't see you. Light a candle and we'll talk."

"There is nothing to talk about. I will not marry you and if I hear so much as a footfall, I will crack you over the head."

"With what?" He sounded wary now.

She hesitated. "With an iron poker."

"You were expecting me, then?"

She heard the astonishment in his voice. He must know that her father could not afford to build a fireplace in her bedchamber, so why would she have a poker? Well, let him think the worst. Perhaps it would frighten him away.

"Yes. It is exactly the sort of wicked trick my father would play to force me to his will."

Actually, this was the one ploy it had never entered her mind that Sir Alun might try, but with the death of Burthred's father and his succession to the barony, Burthred had abandoned his long apathy towards marriage and begun an urgent pursuit of a wife. Christina, however, having eighteen years of neglect to choose another future for herself, had repeatedly refused to see him when he had abruptly come courting her. Like her father, Burthred must have become desperate when he heard that her uncle the abbot was celebrating Christmas in her father's hall. What else could explain his villainous presence in her chamber?

She wished the stick in her hand really *was* made of iron instead of mere wood.

"If you try to touch me, it will be a

sacrilege," she said. "I have dedicated myself to the Holy Church. You risk the punishment of Heaven by assaulting me like this."

"I haven't assaulted you. I can't even see you. And I heard the abbot reproaching your father for not letting you take the vows, so I know you're not dedicated to anyone yet."

"I have dedicated myself in my heart. So just turn around and go back to the hall."

A moment of silence pulsed by, but she heard no move to indicate obedience or defiance.

"I can't go back yet," he said at last. "They will all laugh at me. Your father will call me a spineless, worthless fellow if I don't return with you on my arm."

The beads of the rosary bruised her palms as she clutched the stool's leg tighter. So she had guessed aright. She noticed only now how they conversed with ease, the din of the music having faded to a muffled drumbeat. Her father wanted her cries to be heard by her uncles and aunts and cousins and all the meddlesome neighbors, and most of all by her uncle the abbot. Her uncle would sigh at her weakness when confronted with the temptation of a handsome young man and perform a hasty marriage for the sake of her soul, then return to his abbey without her. She would be forced to live out a dull, hollow life as wife to this brute who colluded with her father to destroy the dream that had burned inside her from the time she had heard her father's chaplain read the Apostles Creed when she had been little more than a toddler.

"'Tis a mortal sin to ravish a nun, Burthred," she warned. "Heaven will never forgive you if you pursue this outrage. Do you wish to spend eternity in a kettle of boiling oil or roasting in a fiery oven or in a field of eternal lice while chattering, fork-tailed demons claw your flesh and laugh at your piteous cries?"

"You are not a nun," he said, with a sad lack of abashed horror in his voice at her description of the hellish fate that awaited him. "And you were betrothed to me first, Meg."

"In the cradle. And my name is Christina. And I don't even *know* you, except for your name."

It was true, and yet she felt like she had known him forever. She could not remember a time when her parents had not talked to her of her Burthred, son of Lord Raymond, and how their houses would one day be joined by marriage.

"Well, that is because you've done nothing but bolt yourself in your chamber every time I asked to see you for the past three months."

"I should have bolted myself in tonight, as well," she said, reflecting bitterly on her carelessness. "Then my virtue would not be at your lecherous mercy."

"If I promised to control my passion, would you agree to light a candle? I feel like I've been struck blind. Did you extinguish the coals in your brazier, too?" His voice sharpened a little

A Candlelight Courting

on the question. "No wonder I feel like I'm standing on a snow bank. You'll catch your death sleeping in this frigid air."

"I will sleep in a colder cell than this in Wilton Abbey. I am strengthening my endurance now for that blessed day."

She heard a sound like stomping feet against the boards of the floor and a huffing breath that might have been an attempt to warm his hands. "Well, I should be glad of even a tiny flame to revive my chilled blood. I will swear my good behavior upon your holy relics if you will only light a candle."

※

A Candlelight Courting is available in print on Amazon, and as e-books on Amazon, Barnes & Noble, and Smashwords. Or order from your favorite bookstore.

Notes

Notes

Printed in Great Britain
by Amazon